Marie Curie

A Brilliant Life

written by Elizabeth MacLeod

Kids Can Press

To Jocelyn, with much love and appreciation
for all she does to make the world a better place

Consultant: Daniela Monaldi, University of Toronto,
Toronto, Ontario, Canada

Acknowledgments: Many thanks to Daniela Monaldi for
making time to review this manuscript. I really appreciate her
efforts and interest in the book. I'm also very grateful to
Prof. Allan Griffin and Larry Avramidis, Department of Physics,
University of Toronto; Dr. David Pantalony, Dartmouth College;
and Julia Naimska, Polish language consultant.

It is a pleasure to be edited by Christine McClymont, an extremely
caring and careful editor. Many thanks for all the time and hard
work that went into the editing. The very creative Karen Powers
has yet again made a fabulous-looking book. I so appreciate the
thoughtfulness and effort that goes into the creation of this series.

Patricia Buckley is also terrific to work with and continues to be
an extremely persistent and skilled photo researcher. I very much
appreciate her talents and hard work. Barbara Spurll has created
wonderful illustrations of Marie that make her come to life.

I'm also grateful to the entire Kids Can Press team, especially
Sheila Barry, Karen Boersma and Valerie Hussey and everyone in
the Technical Services department.

Special thanks to my dad, John and Douglas. And thanks always to
Paul. As Marie Curie said, "… I have the best husband one could
dream of; I could never have imagined finding one like him."

Kids Can Press acknowledges the financial support of the Government of
Ontario, through the Ontario Media Development Corporation's Ontario Book
Initiative; the Ontario Arts Council; the Canada Council for the Arts; and the
Government of Canada, through the BPIDP, for our publishing activity

Published in Canada by
Kids Can Press Ltd.
29 Birch Avenue
Toronto, ON M4V 1E2

Published in the U.S. by
Kids Can Press Ltd.
2250 Military Road
Tonawanda, NY 14150

www.kidscanpress.com

Series editor: Valerie Wyatt
Edited by Christine McClymont
Designed by Karen Powers
Printed and bound in Hong Kong, China, by Book Art Inc., Toronto

The hardcover edition of this book is smyth sewn casebound.
The paperback edition of this book is limp sewn with a drawn-on cover.

CM 04 0 9 8 7 6 5 4 3 2 1
CM PA 04 0 9 8 7 6 5 4 3 2 1

Kids Can Press is a *forus*™ Entertainment company

National Library of Canada Cataloguing in Publication Data

MacLeod, Elizabeth
   Marie Curie : a brilliant life / written by Elizabeth MacLeod.

Includes index.

ISBN 1-55337-570-X (bound).   ISBN 1-55337-571-8 (pbk.)

1. Curie, Marie, 1867–1934– — Juvenile literature. 2. Chemists — Poland —
Biography — Juvenile literature. I. Title.

QD22.C8M32 2004   j540'.92   C2003-907131-6

Contents

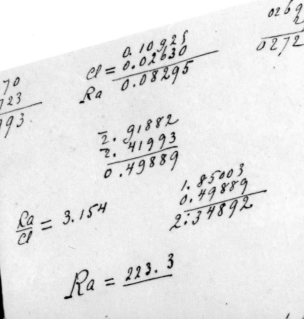

Meet Marie Curie

"Nothing in life is to be feared. It is only to be understood." — Marie

Marie was not only smart, she was also fun — a loyal sister and friend who was always eager for adventure.

Marie was born in Poland, and her last name before she married Pierre Curie was Skłodowska. (Notice the slash through the letter "l"? In Polish, that makes an "l" sound like a "w.") Marie was proud to be the first Polish person to win a Nobel Prize.

If you had passed Marie Curie on the street, you would probably never have known that this small, shy woman was one of the world's most famous scientists. That's the way Marie wanted it. Fame and money meant little to her — science and research were what she thought about.

Marie couldn't understand why people would be interested in her, not just in her work. "In science," she said, "we must be interested in things, not in persons." But Marie led a fascinating life full of breakthrough discoveries, romance, tragedy and achievements.

With her beloved husband, Pierre, Marie discovered and named two new elements, polonium and radium. Together the couple studied radioactivity — Marie was the first person ever to use this word. Marie's discoveries in the field of radiation changed the world. She achieved her goal of using radiation to help people in whatever way possible, especially in the field of medicine. And thanks to Marie, scientists finally understood the atom and its parts.

Not only did Marie win two Nobel prizes in science — she was the first woman to win this top award and the first person to win it twice — but also her research is still very important to many physicists and chemists today. As one of the first women in science, Marie helped open the scientific world to other women. Her daughter, Irène, won a Nobel Prize in chemistry.

How did Marie make her incredible discoveries? Why was she so fascinated by radiation? What was she really like?

M. Curie

At first people were amazed by radiation.
Radioactive material was even added to
makeup for extra sparkle. Today people
know how dangerous radiation can be.

This photo was taken in the dark —
the only light comes from the glow
caused by radium in the dish.

People were fascinated by the most
important woman in science and
wanted to know all about her.

*My goal was to
use radiation to help
people, especially to
improve their health.*

Little Manya

"Do you know, Kazia, in spite of everything I like school. Perhaps you will make fun of me, but nevertheless I must tell you that I like it …"
— Manya

Imagine not being hugged or kissed by your mother! That's what life was like for Marie Curie when she was a little girl in Poland. Marya Skłodowska — Marie's original Polish name, pronounced MAR-ee-ah Squaw-DOFF-ska — was sure her mother loved her. She also knew her mother had tuberculosis (TB). But she didn't understand TB was a serious lung disease that her mother was terrified of passing on to her children.

Manya, as Marya's family called her, was the youngest of five children. Her father taught physics and mathematics in a high school. Manya was fascinated by his scientific instruments — an electroscope (see page 7), glass tubes and scales.

Manya liked school — well, usually. When she started classes in 1874 at the age of six, she was the youngest and smallest. However, she was very smart and memorized things easily, so she was often chosen to recite poems for visitors. Since she was a shy girl, Manya hated this.

Life was tough for many Polish people in the late 1800s. Poland wasn't an independent country as it is now. Warsaw, where Manya lived, was ruled by Russia. Russian laws said that if you spoke Polish or studied Polish history you would be punished harshly. But the laws backfired — they made many Poles, including Manya's family, more proud of their Polish heritage. Manya dreamed of doing wonderful things for her country.

Manya's father was given a lower-paying job because he wasn't pro-Russian enough. Then he lost most of his savings in bad investments. To make ends meet, the family took in boarders. Manya didn't have her own bedroom. Instead, she slept on a sofa in the dining room and got up early so the table could be set for breakfast.

When Manya was eight, her oldest sister, Zofia, caught typhus fever and died. One of the boarders had brought the deadly germs into the house. About two years later, Manya's mother died from tuberculosis. Manya cried her heart out. No one could comfort her for the loss of her mother and sister, two people she loved so much.

Despite her sorrows, Manya was always the best in her class at school. As she neared the end of high school, her family's love and support made her begin to dream of great achievements.

Before Manya was born, her mother, Bronisława Boguska Skłodowska, was director of one of Warsaw's best girls' schools. When money was short, she learned how to make her children's shoes. Manya shared her mother's talent for handwork.

Warsaw

GERMANY   POLAND

ris

ANCE

ITALY

Marie Curie was born in Warsaw, Poland, but spent most of her life in Paris, France.

Manya liked looking at her father's science equipment, including a gold-leaf electroscope like this one. When electricity hits the gold leaves, they fly apart.

Here is Manya's father, Władysław Skłodowski. Notice that his last name is different from Manya's? In Polish, men's last names end in "i" and women's end in "a."

The house where I was born is now a museum. You can visit it —

see page 32.

Here is Manya with her brothers and sisters. They are (left to right) Zofia (the oldest), Helena (second youngest), Manya (the youngest), Józef (second oldest) and Bronisława (the middle child), nicknamed Bronya.

Working girl

"I am learning chemistry from a book … you can imagine how little I get out of that, but what can I do, as I have no place to make experiments or do practical work?" — Marya, writing to her brother Józef

Marya's boyfriend, Kazmierz Zorawski, never forgot her. When he was an old man, he made daily visits to a statue of her in Warsaw.

When Marya (as Manya now called herself) was 15, she finished high school at the top of her class. She was pleased to receive the gold medal but hated shaking hands with the grandmaster of education. After all, he was Russian.

Marya had been working so hard that when school ended she collapsed. Her father sent her to spend a year with family and friends in the country, where she could relax and go to parties. At one ball, she wore through a new pair of dancing slippers!

In 1884, Marya returned to Warsaw and began teaching. She also attended the "Floating University," where students met illegally to study. The school got its name because it had to keep moving to different locations. Polish women couldn't go to university then, so for Marya and her sister Bronya, this was their only chance for more education.

The sisters realized they couldn't learn enough this way to fulfill their ambitions so they made a bargain: Marya would earn money to send Bronya to university in Paris, France, where many Polish people went to study. Then Bronya would pay for Marya to study in Paris.

To earn money, Marya became a governess for the Zorawski family in the village of Szczuki, a small town north of Warsaw. When the oldest boy, Kazmierz, came home from university, he and Marya, now 19, fell in love. But the Zorawskis refused to let their son marry a poor governess. The unhappy couple separated, but Marya kept working for the family because Bronya was depending on her.

To get over her heartbreak, Marya made herself study when she wasn't teaching. She concentrated on physics (the science of energy, force, matter and motion) and chemistry (the science of simple substances and how they combine). But she needed a laboratory for doing experiments.

Marya returned to Warsaw in 1889 and continued working as a governess, tutoring and studying. Luckily for her, a cousin ran Warsaw's Museum of Industry and Agriculture. The name sounds as though it contained farm equipment, and that's what the Russians were supposed to think. Actually, it was a lab where Polish students, including Marya, could study science.

As Marya worked on her experiments, she realized this work suited her. By 1891, when there was enough money for her to join Bronya in Paris, Marya had decided to study physics.

This is the Zorawskis' house, where I was a governess for three years.

Marya (left) is 19 years old in this photo with her sister Bronya. The two were close friends and helped each other all their lives.

Marya drew this sketch of her big brown pointer, Lancet. She brought him along for her year in the country.

Bonjour Paris

"All that I saw and learned that was new delighted me. It was like a new world opened to me, the world of science, which I was at last permitted to know …"
— Marie

One of Marie's classmates drew this portrait of her.

Clutching her luggage and a folding chair, Marya scrambled aboard the train to Paris in the fall of 1891. Traveling as cheaply as possible meant she had no seat for part of the way, so she'd brought her own. Despite her excitement, Marya was sad because she was leaving her beloved father. But she planned to return to Warsaw as soon as she earned her degree in physics.

At first Marie lived with her sister Bronya and her husband. (To fit in better in Paris, Marya used "Marie," the French version of her name.) But their home was an hour from Marie's university, the Sorbonne. As well, Bronya filled her apartment with Polish friends, and their chatter made it hard for Marie to study.

So Marie moved closer to the university, to the cheapest apartment she could find. It was at the top of many stairs, boiling in summer and icy in winter — her basin of water often froze at night. She worked long hours at the school library, mostly so she wouldn't have to heat her apartment. One night Marie was so cold she piled all her clothes *and* her furniture on herself!

Buying and cooking food seemed like a waste of time to Marie, so her meals were often just bread and butter, radishes and tea. Sometimes she fainted from hunger. Then she'd stay with Bronya until she felt better and could get back to studying.

Marie had to work extra hard because she didn't understand French well and her knowledge of physics wasn't as good as her classmates'. Despite these problems, in 1893 Marie earned a master's degree in physics at the Sorbonne. She also got the top marks in her class.

Marie wanted to get another degree, this time in mathematics, but she couldn't afford it. Luckily, she received a scholarship — she later paid it back so another Polish student could use the money — and was able to begin her studies.

Before finishing her math degree, Marie was asked by an organization to study the magnetism of various types of steel. She needed the money so she took the job. But that meant she had to look for a lab. Little did Marie know she was about to find much more than just lab space.

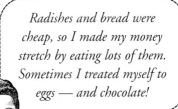

Radishes and bread were cheap, so I made my money stretch by eating lots of them. Sometimes I treated myself to eggs — and chocolate!

Marie worked hard and was very ambitious. Her professors and other students respected her, even though she didn't give them much time to get to know her.

The Sorbonne in Paris is one of the oldest and most famous universities in the world. Marie wanted to study there because she knew she would learn a lot, and because Bronya and many other Polish people lived in Paris.

Paris was an exciting place when Marie arrived there. The Eiffel Tower had just been built and electric streetlights were still very new.

*Ah! How harshly the youth
    of the student passes,
While all around her,
    with passions ever fresh,
Other youths search eagerly
    for easy pleasures!
And yet in solitude
She lives, obscure and blessed,
For in her cell she finds the ardor
That makes her heart immense.*

— poem written by Marie

True love

"My husband and I were so closely united by our affection and our common work that we passed nearly all of our time together."
— Marie

This was Marie's favorite photo of Pierre. He once stayed so late at school discussing physics with his students that they got locked in. They escaped by sliding down a drainpipe — with Pierre talking all the way down.

In 1894, a friend introduced Marie to someone who might help her find lab space. This was Pierre Curie, a teacher and head of the lab at the School of Industrial Physics and Chemistry in Paris. Pierre was already famous for his work with crystals and magnets.

To his surprise, Pierre found himself attracted to Marie. This serious physicist thought most women were a waste of time, but he admired Marie and her love of science. Rather than give her flowers or chocolates, Pierre courted Marie with an autographed copy of one of his physics papers.

Soon after they met, Pierre asked Marie to marry him. Marie didn't know what to say. She loved Pierre but felt that if she married him she would never again live in Poland. When Marie completed her master's degree in math — she finished second in her class — she traveled to Warsaw for a holiday. She wasn't sure she would ever return to Paris.

But Pierre wrote her many love letters. Marie decided to head back to France to continue her education — and to see Pierre again. On July 26, 1895, Marie and Pierre were married. Always practical, Marie wore a dark blue suit she could later wear in the lab.

During her first year of marriage, Marie happily worked in Pierre's lab on her study of steel and magnetism. At the same time, she prepared for an exam that would qualify her to teach science to high-school girls. In August 1896, Marie passed the exam, top of her class, and about a year later finished her steel research. Soon she and Pierre had something else to concentrate on: their baby daughter Irène.

Now Marie decided to earn a doctorate (the highest degree) in physics, and she needed a new topic to study. She had heard about a French physicist named Henri Becquerel and his discovery of mysterious uranium rays in 1896. This new subject fascinated her.

Marie had a hunch that Becquerel's rays were an important clue to the structure of atoms, the basic building blocks of everything in the world. As well, because scientists hadn't done much research on these rays, she wouldn't have to spend a lot of time reading — she could begin working in the lab right away.

Pierre and his brother Jacques, also a physicist, invented the electrometer. This device measures electricity extremely precisely. Marie used it a lot in her work.

While Marie studied the magnetism of different types of steel, Pierre was researching the effect of electricity on crystals.

When one of Marie's cousins gave her money as a wedding present, she bought bicycles. She and Pierre spent their honeymoon happily cycling around the French countryside.

I kept careful notes on everything, from making gooseberry jelly to experimenting in the lab.

The mystery of radiation

"A scientist in his laboratory is not a mere technician: he is also a child confronting natural phenomena that impress him as though they were fairy tales."
— Marie

The discoverer of uranium radiation, Antoine-Henri Becquerel. Radiation is the process of giving off light, heat or other energy. The discovery of radiation was one of the most amazing breakthroughs in physics.

People first heard of mysterious rays in 1895, the year Marie and Pierre were married. A German physicist named Wilhelm Röntgen found that if he passed electricity through a glass tube that had all the air pumped out of it, invisible rays came out. Even though he couldn't see them, the rays left dark smudges on photographic plates (sheets of glass covered with the substance found on modern camera film).

What were these rays — light? particles? Röntgen didn't know, so he called them X rays.

X rays amazed scientists because they could pass through solid materials — such as paper, cloth and skin — that ordinary light couldn't. For the first time, people could see skeletons inside living bodies. Doctors started using X rays to examine patients. Meanwhile, physicists searched for the source that produced this new kind of radiation.

In Paris, Henri Becquerel was fascinated by Röntgen's work. He had been studying phosphorescent materials (substances that go on glowing after being exposed to light), and he wondered if these materials also gave off X rays. So he put samples of phosphorescent materials on photographic plates wrapped in thick black paper and exposed them to sunlight.

None of Becquerel's samples left dark smudges on the photographic plates the way Röntgen's X rays did — except a rock containing uranium. The uranium rock seemed to produce some kind of invisible rays that could pass through thick black paper.

Becquerel repeated the experiment. He wrapped a photographic plate in black paper and placed a metal cross between the paper and the uranium rock. But Paris was cloudy in February 1896, so he put everything away in a dark cupboard to wait for some sunshine.

After a few days, Becquerel got tired of waiting and developed the photographic plate anyway. He was amazed when an image of the cross showed up on the plate! This meant the uranium rock had given off rays without being exposed to sunlight. Becquerel had found another new kind of radiation. But when he couldn't find a link between phosphorescence and uranium rays, he lost interest.

Most other scientists ignored Becquerel's uranium rays, too. But not Marie Curie.

Becquerel's photographic plate showing the fog left around a cross by uranium rays. If you look carefully you can see the outline of the cross as well as some of Becquerel's notes.

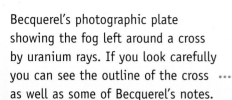

Here's the first-ever X-ray image, showing Wilhelm Röntgen's wife's hand. People all over the world were astounded by X rays. Some even began taking baths fully clothed so no one would use X rays to peek through walls at them!

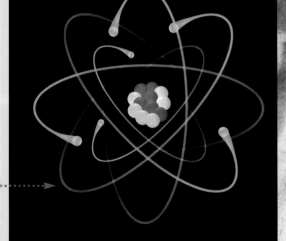

I was fascinated by radiation and couldn't wait to begin studying it.

In this carbon atom you can see its core (nucleus) circled by smaller particles called electrons. Marie would discover that radiation is linked to reactions in atoms.

Glass tubes filled with special gas helped Henri Becquerel study phosphorescent materials. By shooting electricity through a crystal like this pink one, he could tell if it gave off radiation.

Marie's discoveries

"... the radiation that I could not explain comes from a new chemical element. The element is there and I've got to find it." — Marie

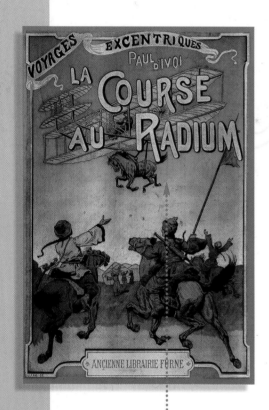

La Course au Radium was one of many science fiction books that featured radium as an incredible cure for disease, an amazing source of power or a dangerous weapon.

When Marie began studying uranium, she knew it was one of 70 elements chemists had discovered. (An element is a substance, such as gold or oxygen, composed of only one type of atom.) Could she find uranium-type rays coming from other elements? One by one, she checked — and found that the element thorium also gave off rays.

Next, Marie analyzed rocks that contained more than one element. As she expected, most of the uranium-type rays were given off by the rocks called pitchblende. This was because they contained uranium or thorium. But to Marie's surprise, pitchblende gave off more radiation than she expected. She knew she wasn't wrong — she'd checked her results 20 times. What was causing this extra radiation?

Pierre decided to join Marie in her work. He agreed that no known elements besides uranium and thorium gave off the unusual rays. There was only one explanation for the extra radiation in pitchblende. In July 1898, Marie announced her discovery — she had found a new element, which she named polonium after her beloved Poland. She also invented the word "radioactive" to describe polonium, uranium and thorium.

In December 1898, Marie announced the discovery of another new, even more radioactive, element — radium. But years of work lay ahead. Marie and Pierre had to prove to fellow scientists that polonium and radium existed. To do this, they had to produce the two elements in their purest forms, find the weight of their atoms, and show that each element had an atomic weight different from any other element's.

Marie and Pierre decided to focus first on trying to produce pure radium. They needed two things: lots of pitchblende and a large lab. The main pitchblende source was a mine in Austria that dumped its waste rock — what Marie wanted — in a nearby forest. Thanks to a friend, Marie and Pierre were able to buy huge amounts of pitchblende very cheaply. When they opened the bags, out poured pine needles, too!

Finding lab space was harder. The only room available was a cold, leaky shed near Pierre's work, but it gave Marie and Pierre the space they needed. Marie had to melt pitchblende in huge pots and stir it with a steel rod almost as tall as she was. Despite the hard work, she was determined to discover all she could about radioactivity.

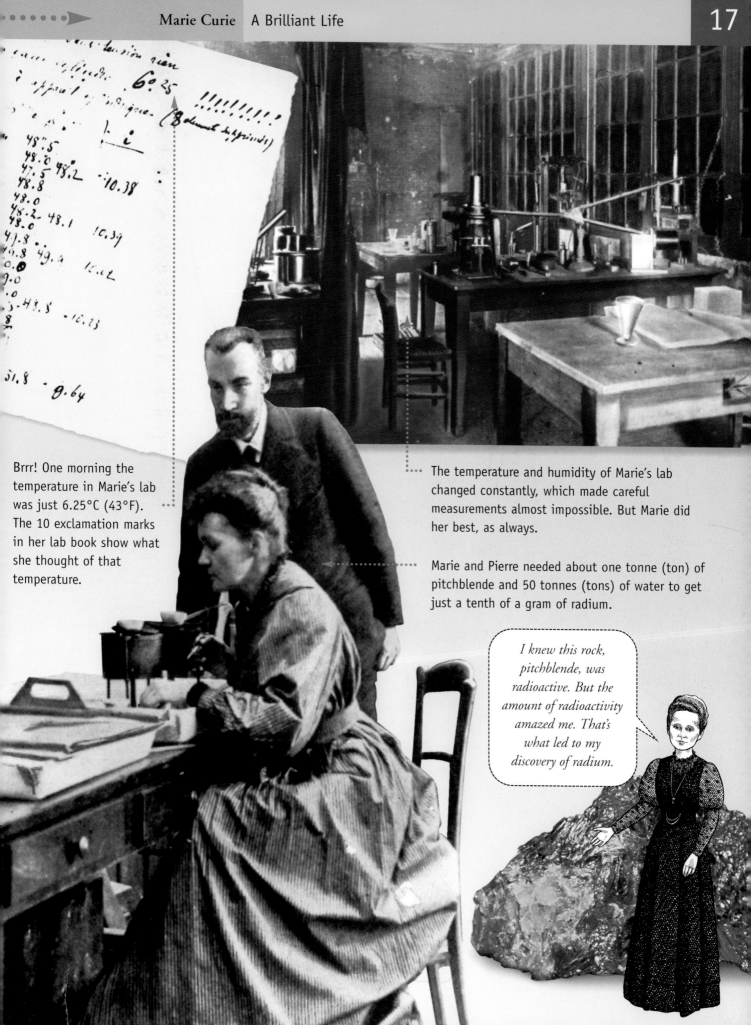

Brrr! One morning the temperature in Marie's lab was just 6.25°C (43°F). The 10 exclamation marks in her lab book show what she thought of that temperature.

The temperature and humidity of Marie's lab changed constantly, which made careful measurements almost impossible. But Marie did her best, as always.

Marie and Pierre needed about one tonne (ton) of pitchblende and 50 tonnes (tons) of water to get just a tenth of a gram of radium.

I knew this rock, pitchblende, was radioactive. But the amount of radioactivity amazed me. That's what led to my discovery of radium.

Brilliant breakthrough

"One of our pleasures was to enter our workshop at night; then, all around us, we would see the luminous silhouettes of the beakers and capsules that contained our products."
— Marie

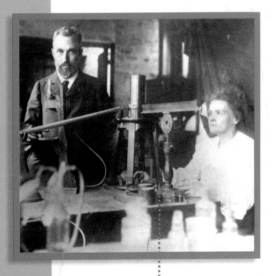

It took Marie and Pierre almost four years (from 1898 to 1902) to establish that radium was a new element. With a better lab, Marie felt that they could have done it in a year.

Although Marie and Pierre lived extremely cheaply, by 1900 they had real money troubles. Pierre needed a well-paying job but he wasn't good at talking to the higher-up professors who could help him — he'd rather be working in his lab. So Pierre had to take a job teaching high-school students. What a comedown for such a famous scientist!

Marie resented how the French universities treated her husband. But when a university in Geneva, Switzerland, offered him a good job, the couple turned it down. They felt the move would delay Marie's work. Luckily, the Swiss offer made the Paris universities realize Pierre's value, and the Sorbonne finally hired him as a lecturer.

Between 1900 and 1903, Marie published many reports on her work. That's amazing, because she was also finishing her doctoral degree and trying to produce pure radium. As well, in October 1900, Marie began teaching at a teachers' college in Sèvres, a suburb of Paris. She liked working with the bright young women who were studying to teach high-school girls. Marie became a wonderful teacher and her pupils grew to love her.

In the lab, Marie continued her grueling work with pitchblende until she was able to produce one-tenth of a gram of radium. On July 21, 1902, she finally reported the weight of one radium atom — a major breakthrough! Because the weight of the radium atom was different from the atomic weight of any other element, it proved that Marie had discovered a new element (every element has a different atomic weight).

Marie and Pierre could have become rich by claiming all rights to working with radium. But instead they shared their information, telling how they'd purified the element, and more. They believed scientific research should benefit everyone. Marie and Pierre may also never have dreamed how valuable radium could become.

By June 1903, Marie was ready for the last step to getting her doctorate in physics: an exam where she met with senior professors and answered questions about her research. Marie was still shy about speaking in public, but no one, not even these experts, knew more than she did about radiation. She earned top marks and became the first woman in Europe to receive a doctorate in science.

Marie worked hard to measure the exact weight of radium. In these lab notes, she measured it as 223.3. Today we know it's 226, which means each radium atom weighs 226 times as much as a hydrogen atom.

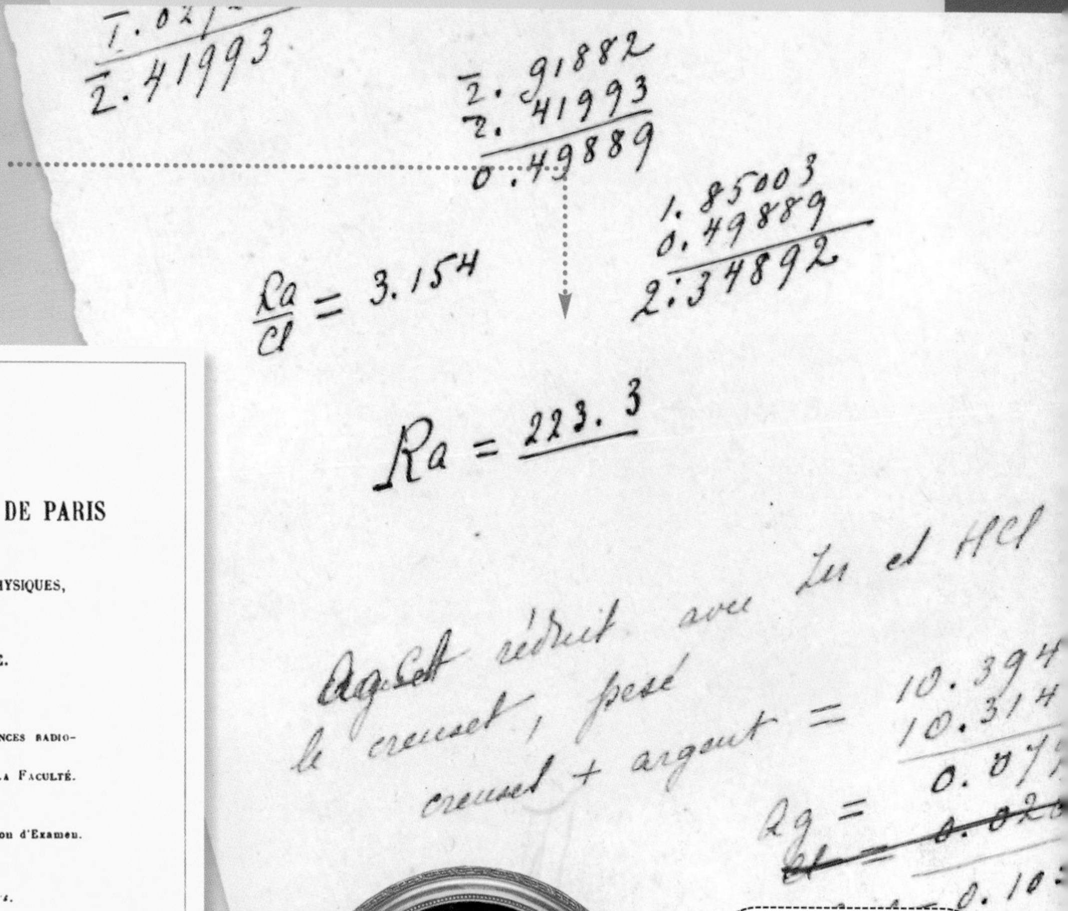

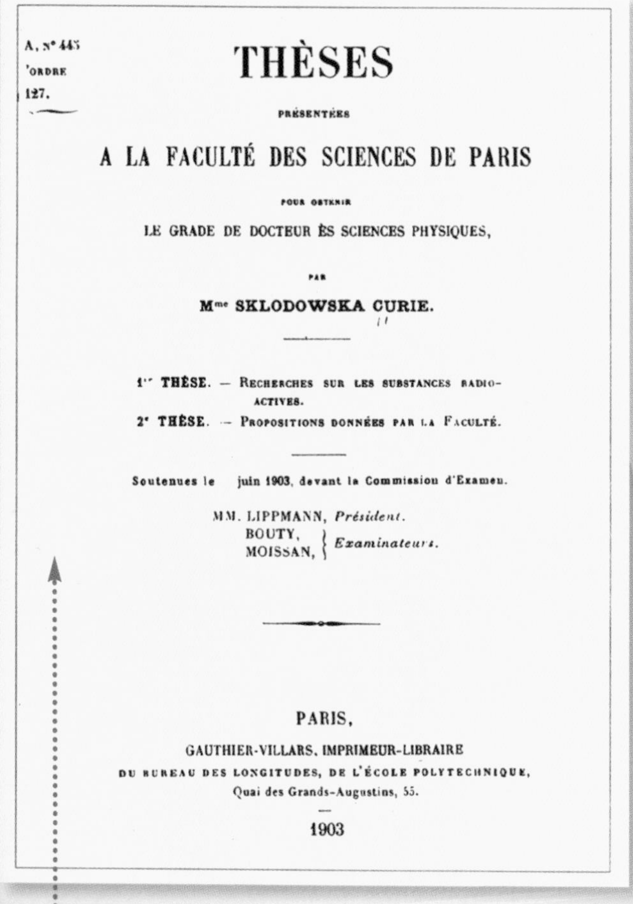

2.41993
2.91882
2.41993
0.49889
1.85003
0.49889
2.34892
Ra/Cl = 3.154
Ra = 223.3

A, n° 445
ORDRE
127.

THÈSES

PRÉSENTÉES

A LA FACULTÉ DES SCIENCES DE PARIS

POUR OBTENIR

LE GRADE DE DOCTEUR ÈS SCIENCES PHYSIQUES,

PAR

Mme SKLODOWSKA CURIE.

1re THÈSE. — Recherches sur les substances radioactives.

2e THÈSE. — Propositions données par la Faculté.

Soutenues le juin 1903, devant la Commission d'Examen.

MM. LIPPMANN, *Président.*
BOUTY, MOISSAN, } *Examinateurs.*

PARIS,

GAUTHIER-VILLARS, IMPRIMEUR-LIBRAIRE
DU BUREAU DES LONGITUDES, DE L'ÉCOLE POLYTECHNIQUE,
Quai des Grands-Augustins, 55.

1903

Experts said Marie's doctoral paper, "Research on Radioactive Substances," was the greatest contribution to science ever made by such a report. It led to the beginnings of a new branch of science — nuclear physics.

Pierre and I worked long hours in our lab. Our daughter Irène was often cared for by Pierre's father, whom she loved.

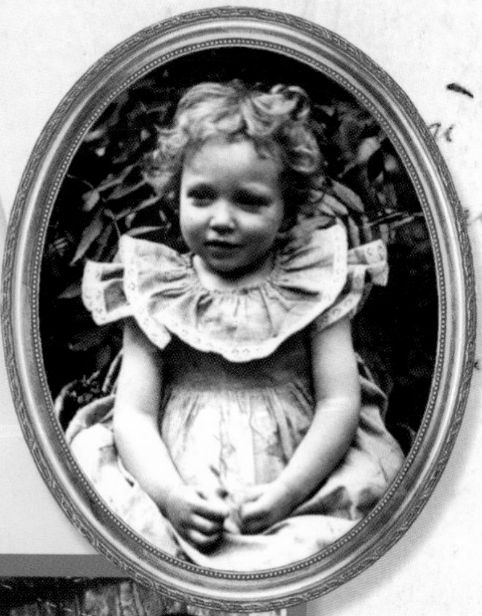

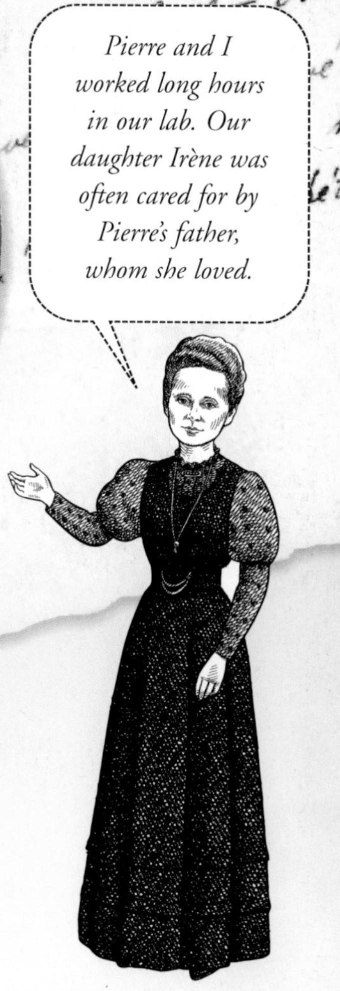

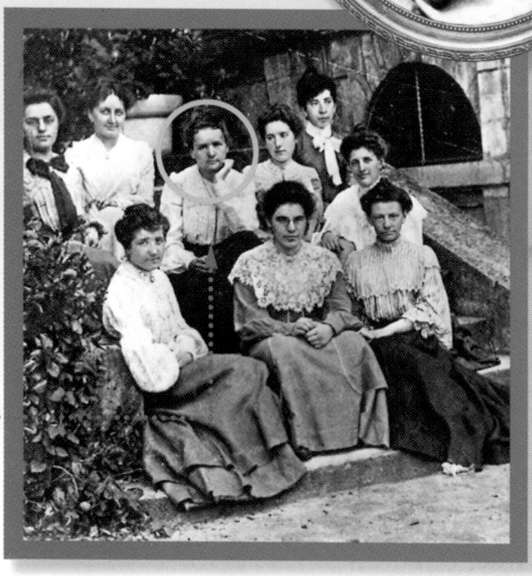

Marie was the first woman to teach at the École Normale Supérieure de Sèvres. Here she is with some of her students.

World famous

"Life is not easy for any of us. But what of that? We must have perseverance and, above all, confidence in ourselves. We must believe that we are gifted for something and that this thing must be attained." — Marie

I was delighted when my daughter Ève was born in December 1904. The girls called me "Mé" and Pierre "Pé." In this photo, Ève is one year old and Irène is eight.

While Marie continued working on radium, Pierre was unable to do much research. He was always exhausted and in pain. He and Marie thought this was because he was just too busy lecturing, working in the lab and helping care for their daughter Irène.

But Marie was always tired also. As well, she had a miscarriage and lost a lot of weight. Both Pierre and Marie had burnt, numb fingertips. Today, we know that overexposure to radioactivity, such as radium rays, can cause these problems. Did Marie and Pierre ignore this possibility?

It's hard to believe these two experts didn't realize the effect radium was having on them. Marie and Pierre knew that exposing their skin to the radioactive radium for just a few hours caused a "burn" that took months to heal — Pierre had tried this as an experiment.

But radium had benefits too. Because it could kill healthy tissue, doctors tested it on diseased cells and found it also destroyed them. Soon radium was being used to stop cancer cells from growing in patients with cancer. The new treatment was called "Curietherapy."

Despite their health problems, the year ended well for Marie and Pierre. They finally began to receive the recognition they deserved. In November 1903, they were given the Humphry Davy Medal, England's highest award in chemistry. But Marie and Pierre's lives really changed in December when, with Henri Becquerel, they won the Nobel Prize for physics. The Nobel Prize is one of the world's top science awards.

Marie was proud to be the first Polish person to win this prize. The Nobel came with a cash award so, for the first time, the Curies could afford a lab assistant. Reporters and visitors wanted to meet the famous scientists — writers even tried to interview the Curies' young daughter and their cat!

Nobel Prize winners had to travel to Sweden to receive their award and speak about their work. Marie was too ill to go, but Pierre wanted her to attend the ceremony and get the credit she deserved. It wasn't until 1905, when she felt well enough, that they went to Sweden and received the prize.

Thanks to the Nobel Prize, Pierre was made a professor at the Sorbonne University in October 1904. Marie happily became the head of Pierre's laboratory. Now Marie was earning a salary for her scientific work, and she and Pierre finally had proper lab space.

Pierre heard ahead of time that he and Henri
Becquerel might win the Nobel Prize, but there
was no mention of Marie. Pierre said he wouldn't
accept the award unless they shared it with her.
He and Marie received a medal and this certificate.

These "Sparklets" are
bulbs full of radon, the
gas produced by radium.
They were added to
water to make it
sparkle. Now
people know
how dangerous
this was.

Marie's hands became badly
scarred from radiation
poisoning. Irène is
pointing to the marks.

Sometimes Pierre's pain caused him
to moan all night. Marie could do
nothing but listen anxiously and try
to keep young Irène from hearing.

Tragedy!

*"My dear Pierre,
I want you to know that
… the irises are coming
out. You would have
loved them. I want you
to know too that I've
been appointed to your
[job] and some people
have been mad enough
to congratulate me."*
— Marie

This was Pierre's favorite photo
of Marie. She had a copy of it
buried with him and placed
blue periwinkle flowers (above)
on his coffin.

The Curie family spent a wonderful weekend in the country in mid-April 1906. They strolled through the woods and fields, chasing butterflies and picking wildflowers. Pierre took a bouquet of periwinkles home to Paris when he had to return ahead of his family.

A few days later, the whole family was home, rushing through a normal, busy day. Pierre was running errands on the rain-soaked streets when he stepped out to cross the road and fell in front of a horse-drawn wagon.

Startled, the huge horses reared up. Their hooves missed Pierre as they came down and, amazingly, so did the wagon's front wheels. But the rear wheels crushed Pierre's skull. When word spread that a famous scientist had been killed, the crowd had to be stopped from attacking the innocent driver.

Marie didn't hear about the tragedy until she returned home that night. Because Pierre had never wanted honors, Marie held his funeral quickly, before the government got involved. Instead of the usual black cloth, she placed periwinkles on the coffin as a reminder of their last happy weekend.

Less than a month after Pierre's death, Marie was offered his job at the Sorbonne. She'd be the first woman to lecture at the university in its 650-year history. Marie accepted, but she felt Pierre's death was a high price to pay for this honor. Before her first class, reporters, students and curious people crowded the hall. Would Marie praise her husband? Would she break down? Instead, Marie quietly began speaking — at the very spot where Pierre had left off.

One of Marie's deepest regrets was that Pierre had died without ever having his own permanent lab. It gave her great satisfaction when, in 1909, plans were begun to establish the Radium Institute in Paris. It would have a laboratory that Marie would supervise, to be called the Curie Pavilion.

The Radiology Congress, an international group of radiation scientists, decided they needed a new unit of measurement for amounts of radiation — and they would call it the "curie." Marie insisted she was the only one who could take on the task of working out the exact size of a curie unit. It was painstaking work, but she did it in Pierre's honor.

The streets of Paris became very slick when it rained. No wonder poor Pierre slipped as he hurried through his busy day.

Marie was devastated by Pierre's death. But years earlier he had said to her, "Whatever happens, even if one should become like a body without a soul, still one must always work."

When Pierre died, the French government offered Marie an allowance. Marie refused, saying she could look after herself and her daughters.

I rarely spoke my husband's name after he died, and I found it hard to talk about him with Irène and Ève.

Tough times

"Marie Curie is, of all celebrated beings, the one whom fame has not corrupted."
— Albert Einstein

After a long illness, Marie was finally able to travel to Birmingham, England, in 1913 to receive an honorary degree.

I hated attending award ceremonies with their speeches and photo sessions — I was always happier in my lab.

In 1911 Marie's friends convinced her to think about becoming a member of the French Academy of Sciences. Marie wasn't interested in the honor but she knew it would help her get money for research and jobs.

This was the first time a woman had tried to become a member of the famous Academy and the Paris newspapers went wild. Many were against her — not only was Marie a woman, they said, but she was also a foreigner, not French. In the end, Marie lost by two votes and felt angry and humiliated.

Outside France, Marie was more appreciated. She was invited to the first gathering of the world's top physicists, the Solvay Congress, in Brussels, Belgium. At this conference, Marie met Albert Einstein. He liked Marie because, like him, she was more interested in science than fame.

While Marie was in Brussels, news of a scandal involving her and another physicist hit the newspapers. Paul Langevin, who was also at the conference, had been a good friend of Pierre and Marie's, and Marie cared deeply for him. Paul's wife claimed they were in love with each other. Although Paul and his wife were already separated, Marie was criticized for being a foreigner and for breaking up a French family.

When Marie returned to Paris, crowds hurled insults at her. Duels were fought between her supporters and her critics. Marie's family urged her to return to Poland, but Pierre's brother, Jacques, supported her. Marie wanted to stay in France both for her children's sake and to see the Radium Institute completed.

Just after the Langevin scandal broke, Marie received amazing news — she'd won a second Nobel Prize, this time in chemistry. Marie was the first person ever to win more than one of these top awards. But she was so disliked in France that some people tried to stop her from receiving it.

Whether from radiation sickness or from worry, Marie's health became very poor. Soon after receiving her Nobel, she was rushed to hospital and was ill for more than a year. In July 1913, she was able to take her daughters on a holiday with Albert Einstein and his son Hans in the Swiss Alps. Marie enjoyed herself but was anxious to return to Paris. She wanted to keep an eye on the building of the Radium Institute.

Marie was given this medal when she received her second Nobel Prize for her discovery of radium. The Nobel committee said her work had changed scientists' understanding of the atom and had opened up new areas of medicine.

At the Solvay Congress in 1911, Marie looks over a paper with Henri Poincaré, who had worked with Pierre. Paul Langevin is on the far right, with Albert Einstein beside him.

Paul Langevin appreciated being able to discuss physics with Marie. Many years later, Marie's granddaughter Hélène would marry Paul's grandson, Michel.

There was so little radium in the early 1900s that it was extremely expensive. The cost of building the entire Radium Institute was only a little more than the cost of a gram of radium.

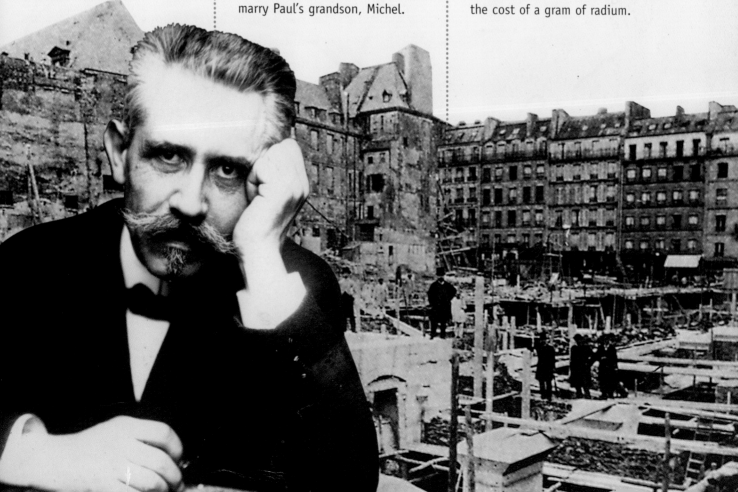

On the battlefield

"I am resolved to put all my strength at the service of my adopted country, since I cannot do anything for my unfortunate native country just now, bathed as it is in blood after more than a century of suffering."
— Marie

Although Irène was only 17, she joined her mother in the fall of 1914 on the front lines. The two women operated the X-ray machines and lived like soldiers.

Before the Radium Institute could open in August 1914, World War I broke out. France, Poland and other countries were soon under attack. Marie finally had the laboratory she and Pierre had dreamed of, but nothing could be done with it. Most of her staff were men so they were called away to fight.

Although Marie was horrified by the war, she was determined to help France. She knew X rays would be very useful, letting doctors see bullets and broken bones in wounded soldiers. But most Paris hospitals knew little about X rays and had no equipment. So Marie persuaded manufacturers and labs to give the hospitals any X-ray equipment they had.

Marie soon realized soldiers would be helped more if the X-ray equipment was closer to the battlefields. But how could she get it there? Cars were the answer. It was difficult, but eventually Marie collected a fleet of 20 cars, which became known as *petites Curies* or "little Curies." Each was equipped with X-ray equipment and a generator to power it. Marie and a team of volunteers, including her daughter Irène, drove them to the front lines.

At first, some army doctors thought X-ray technology was useless, and the wounded soldiers wondered if X rays would hurt. Soon they all understood how useful the equipment was and how it helped doctors diagnose injuries quickly.

When France asked its citizens to donate their gold and silver to help the war effort, Marie offered all her medals, including her Nobel prizes. The government was grateful but returned the valuable medals to her. Marie then began teaching other women how to use the X-ray equipment so more X-ray units could be driven close to the battlefields.

Meanwhile, another scientist discovered how to use radon, the radioactive gas given off by radium, to heal wounds. It was easier to use than radium and less dangerous. Marie donated the radon gas created at the Radium Institute to the army hospitals in Paris.

When the war finally ended in November 1918, Marie was delighted. Not only had France's side won, but also her beloved Poland had finally become a free, independent country. Irène received a military medal for her hospital work — but not Marie. Perhaps some people had still not forgotten the Langevin scandal.

In her *petite Curie*, Marie visited almost 400 hospitals during World War I. She set up 200 X-ray rooms in which more than 1 million X-ray photos were taken.

Marie taught 150 women how to use X-ray machines. They helped get the technology to the battlefields where it was needed. Her students ranged from maids to upper-class ladies.

I traveled to many battlefields during the war, but I always wrote postcards and letters to keep in touch with Irène and Ève.

CARTE POSTALE

CORRESPONDANCE

Marie's lasting impact

"One never notices what has been done; one can only see what remains to be done." — Marie

With the war behind her, Marie could finally do experiments at the Radium Institute, in the first lab that was really her own. How she wished Pierre could share it with her.

Marie had given most of her money to France during the war, so she had little left to buy radium for research. But an American writer, Missy Meloney, was very impressed by Marie. She encouraged American women to donate $100 000 to buy a gram of radium for the Radium Institute. In 1921, Marie visited the United States to receive this valuable gift.

In the early 1920s scientists finally realized the dangers of radiation. People working with radioactive material began taking precautions. But it was too late for Marie. Her work with radiation probably caused the cataracts in her eyes that now threatened her with blindness. She had four operations to remove the cataracts but wanted no one to know — she didn't want people to think she was old and helpless.

Marie's next ten years were filled with achievements. She was delighted to help Poland by opening the Warsaw Radium Institute there in 1925 with her sister Bronya as director. Marie continued working at the Radium Institute in Paris, and now her daughter Irène and Irène's husband, Frédéric Joliot, worked with her.

American women donated another gram of radium in 1929, and again Marie crossed the ocean to receive it. But in 1934 she became very ill. Marie died in July from aplastic anemia, a lack of red blood cells, caused by long exposure to radiation.

Marie always feared that radium and other radioactive materials would eventually be turned into weapons. She was right — American scientists used uranium to create atomic bombs in 1945. The bombs were dropped on Hiroshima and Nagasaki, Japan, at the end of World War II, and hundreds of thousands of people died.

But scientists have discovered that radiation also has many benefits. Radiation therapy is one of the few effective treatments for cancer. Today scientists use radiation to produce electricity, kill organisms that spoil food, find weak spots in bridges or pipelines and detect smoke in homes.

Marie amazed the world with her discoveries and made people look at science and scientists differently. Marie also showed that through hard work and determination anything is possible.

One of the high points of Marie's 1921 tour of the United States was meeting President Warren G. Harding at the White House. On behalf of the women of America, he presented Marie with a gram of radium.

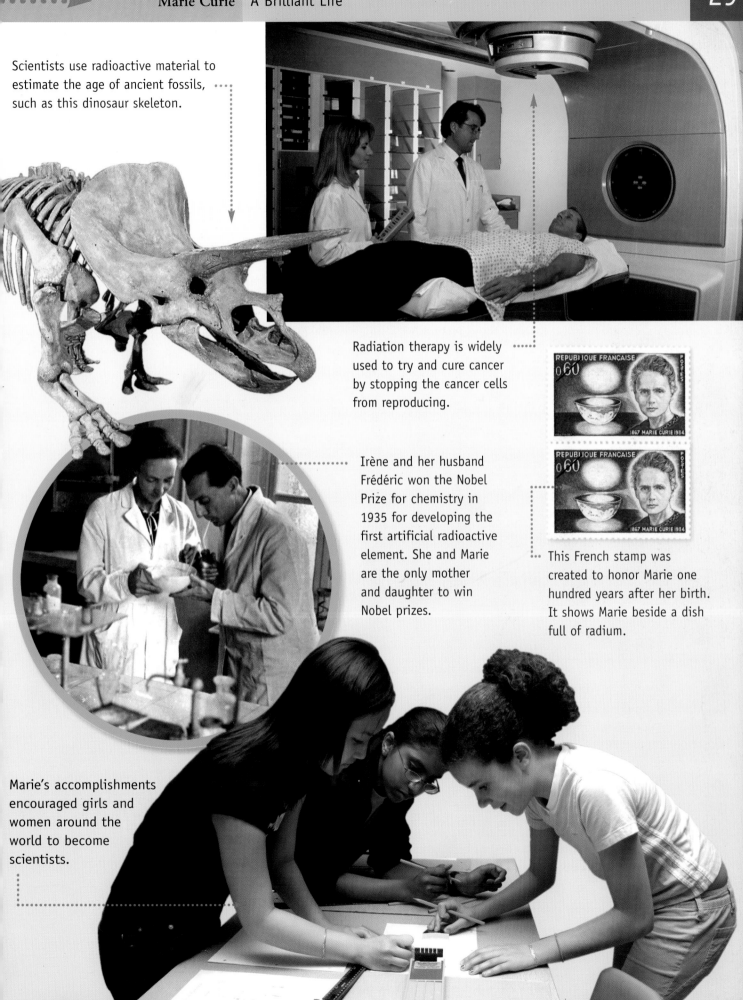

Scientists use radioactive material to estimate the age of ancient fossils, such as this dinosaur skeleton.

Radiation therapy is widely used to try and cure cancer by stopping the cancer cells from reproducing.

Irène and her husband Frédéric won the Nobel Prize for chemistry in 1935 for developing the first artificial radioactive element. She and Marie are the only mother and daughter to win Nobel prizes.

This French stamp was created to honor Marie one hundred years after her birth. It shows Marie beside a dish full of radium.

Marie's accomplishments encouraged girls and women around the world to become scientists.

Marie's life at a glance

1859 May 15 — Pierre Curie is born in Paris, France

1867 November 7 — Marya Salomea Skłodowska is born in Warsaw, Poland

1873 Marya's family begins to have money troubles

1876 January — Marya's sister Zofia dies of typhus fever

1878 May — Marya's mother dies of tuberculosis

1883 Marya graduates from high school, earning a gold medal as top student. She then takes a year off in the country.

1884 Marya returns to Warsaw and studies at the "Floating University"

1885 Marya and her sister Bronya work as governesses to earn money for university in Paris. Bronya goes first to become a doctor.

1886 Marya becomes a governess for the Zorawski family in Szczuki, Poland. She falls in love with the family's oldest son but his parents refuse to let the couple marry.

1889 Marya returns to Warsaw and continues working as a governess, tutoring and studying

1891 Marya leaves for Paris to join Bronya and study science at the Sorbonne university. She begins using the French form of her name, Marie.

1892 Marie moves out of Bronya's house to live closer to the university

1893 Marie places first in her class and obtains a university degree in physics. She is the first woman to earn this honor at the Sorbonne.

1894 Marie meets Pierre Curie while looking for lab space to do research in the magnetism of various types of steel. She earns a second degree, this one in math.

1895 July 26 — Marie marries Pierre

1896 August — Marie receives her certificate to teach girls in high school

1897 September 12 — Irène Curie is born

Marie begins her research into radioactivity as she studies to earn a doctorate in physics

1898 July 18 — Marie and Pierre announce the discovery of the element polonium and first use the word "radioactivity"

December 26 — Marie, Pierre and assistant Gustave Bémont announce the discovery of radium

1899 Marie begins the process of isolating radium from pitchblende

1900 Pierre becomes a lecturer at the Sorbonne

October — Marie begins teaching at the École Normale Supérieure de Sèvres, the first woman to teach there

1902 July 21 — Marie proves that radium is a new element

1903 June 25 — Marie receives a doctorate for her work on radioactivity, becoming the first woman in Europe to earn this degree

August — Marie has a miscarriage

November — Marie and Pierre are awarded the Humphry Davy Medal by the Royal Society of London

December — Marie, Pierre and Henri Becquerel share the Nobel Prize for physics for their work on radioactivity

Marie becomes the first woman, and the first Polish person, to be awarded a Nobel Prize

1904 December 6 — Ève Denise Curie is born

Pierre is appointed professor at the Sorbonne. Marie becomes the head of his lab there.

1905 June — Marie and Pierre travel to Sweden to receive their Nobel Prize (Marie was too sick to attend the award ceremony in 1903)

1906 April 19 — Pierre is killed when he's run over by a horse-drawn wagon

November 5 — Marie takes over Pierre's classes and becomes the first woman to teach at the Sorbonne

1909 Work begins on the Radium Institute in Paris. It will have a lab named the Curie Pavilion in Pierre's honor.

1910 The Radiology Congress chooses the curie as the basic unit of radioactivity

1911 October — Marie attends the first Solvay Congress in Brussels, Belgium, and becomes friends with Albert Einstein

November 4 — Marie is accused of having a love affair with Paul Langevin and the scandal makes her very unpopular in France

November 7 — Marie wins the Nobel Prize for chemistry for her work on radium. She becomes the first person to receive two Nobel prizes.

1912 Marie is made Director of the Radium Institute in Paris

1914 August 4 — World War I breaks out

August — The Radium Institute opens just after World War I begins

1914–1918 Marie organizes mobile X-ray units for the war and trains 150 operators

1918 November 11 — World War I ends

Marie's daughter Irène begins working in her mother's lab at the Radium Institute

1921 May 20 — U.S. President Warren G. Harding presents Marie with a gram of radium for the Radium Institute on behalf of American women

May–June — Marie tours the United States, raising funds for research

1924 Frédéric Joliot begins working with Marie and Irène

1926 October 9 — Irène marries Frédéric

1929 Marie returns to the United States to receive funds for another gram of radium

1934 January 15 — Marie's daughter and son-in-law, Irène and Frédéric Joliot-Curie, announce their discovery of artificial radioactivity

July 4 — Marie Curie dies of aplastic anemia caused by radiation poisoning

1935 Irène and Frédéric receive the Nobel Prize for chemistry

1995 April 20 — Marie and Pierre are reburied in the Panthéon in Paris, France. She is the first woman given that honor based on her own achievements.

When I began my research into radiation, I never dreamed I'd spend the rest of my life working on it.

Visit Marie

Le Musée Curie (Curie Museum),
11 rue Pierre et Marie Curie, Paris

Marie's workplace has been turned into a museum. Her lab furniture and books are still radioactive, so they've been replaced with replicas. See displays on Marie and Pierre's work, as well as Irène and Frédéric's.

Museum of Maria Skłodowska-Curie,
16 Freta St., Warsaw, Poland

You can tour this house where Marie was born, and see her letters, lab equipment and other belongings.

Long Island Museum of Science and Technology, Long Island, New York

Find out more about Marie and other women who have contributed to the study of nuclear science. You'll also learn about natural radioactivity in everyday items.

National Atomic Museum,
1905 Mountain Road NW, Albuquerque, New Mexico

This is a museum about nuclear science and its history. You can see displays on pioneers in the field — including Marie Curie and Albert Einstein — as well as current and future developments in the uses of nuclear technology.

You can find out more about me and my work at all of these museums. You can visit some of them on the Web, too.

Index